FINGERPRINT SCIENCE
How to Roll, Classify, File and Use Fingerprints

CLARENCE GERALD COLLINS

THOMSON
™
WADSWORTH

Australia • Canada • Mexico • Singapore • Spain
United Kingdom • United States

ISBN: 0-942728-18-1
Library of Congress Catalog Number: 84-73191

Wadsworth/Thomson Learning
10 Davis Drive
Belmont CA 94002-3098
USA

For information about our products, contact us:
Thomson Learning Academic Resource Center
1-800-423-0563
http://www.wadsworth.com

For permission to use material from this text or product,
submit a request online at http://www.thomsonrights.com

Any additional questions about permissions can be
submitted by email to thomsonrights@thomson.com

Printed in the United States of America
10 9 8 7 6 5

DEDICATION

This book is dedicated to my late son, Stephen Christopher Collins, who will always live in my heart.

— *Clarence Gerald Collins*

ACKNOWLEDGEMENT

I wish to express my sincere appreciation to the Federal Bureau of Investigation, United States Department of Justice, for the use of material and diagrams from their publication, *The Science of Fingerprints.*

PREFACE

About the text...

This text is designed for the beginning and intermediate fingerprint classifier. It will also serve as an excellent quick references source for the more experienced technician.

The book's purpose is to present, in an easily understood manner, specific material dealing with all phases of fingerprint classification, identification, and filing systems.

About the author...

Mr. Collins is retired from the Los Angeles County Sheriff's Department after 31 years of service. Throughout the majority of his career he was assigned to the Scientific Services Bureau, Latent Fingerprint Unit. He is a member of the International Association for Identification and the Southern California Association of Fingerprint Officers.

The author holds a life-time teaching credential and is a recognized lecturer and authority on the science of fingerprints.

Cases Involving Fingerprint Evidence

There is no doubt that law enforcement agencies throughout the world can cite case examples of outstanding accomplishments by their latent print technicians. For illustration purposes, three cases involving a police department's Latent Print Section are cited below.

The first was a series of burglary-murders, wherein the suspect was finally placed on a burglary-murder scene by a partial palm print developed on the inside wooden wall of a milk delivery door. The opening was seemingly too small for a child to get through, let alone a six foot, 200 pound burglar. The suspect wore leather gloves, laid on his back and pushed himself backwards through the chute to enter the apartment. As he did so, his right-hand glove became unbuttoned allowing his palm to touch the wooden surface and leave a print. He was convicted and executed for murder.

The second example involved a series of bar robberies and a murder wherein one of the suspects made a series of purchases with a Sears Roebuck credit card stolen from one of the victims. When the sales slips were obtained from Sears, it was determined that 38 persons had handled the slips during the credit processing. Notwithstanding this discouraging factor, the print technician tenaciously processed the slips via chemical methods and developed seven latent prints left by the suspect when he handled and signed the slips. He was convicted of murder and robbery.

The third case was a sexual assault and strangulation murder of a housewife by a T.V. serviceman. His partial palm print, developed on the lower portion of a wall in a hallway next to where the victim was found, broke his story that he was never in that part of the house. This evidence was a major factor in his trial and he was convicted of murder.

Table of Contents

We all live under the same sky,
but we don't all have the same horizon.

— *Konrad Adenauer*

Chapter 1

Fingerprints:
Their History and Meaning

From the earliest times the use of fingerprints, as a mark of specific identity, appears to have acquired acceptance along with the customs of tattooing, clipping, branding and cutting. The ridges and depressions on the tips of the fingers aroused sufficient interest in prehistoric man to be included among his carvings on the stone cliffs of Nova Scotia and the Petroglyphs found on Gavrinis Island off the Northwest coast of France. China is credited with utilizing fingerprints (about 200 B.C.) as a mark of identification. The Chinese successfully applied this facility in their business and legal enterprises as early as the 11th century.

In 1684, Dr. Nehemiah Drew published a report of fingerprint observations made in London, England describing the ridges and pores of the hands and feet. In 1686, Marcello Malpighi published a book on his study of pores and ridges. His research work was of such outstanding importance that one of the layers of the human skin now bears his name.

In 1823, Johannes E. Purkinje published a thesis describing fingerprint types. He classified them into nine major groups. In 1858, Sir William Herschel, employed by the East India Company, printed the palms of natives in order to avoid impersonation among the laborers. Prints of the entire palm were used instead of signatures. In 1880, Dr. Henry Faulds, stationed at

Tsukiji Hospital in Japan, wrote on the subject of fingerprints. He advocated their use in identifying criminals.

In 1891, Juan Vucetich, an Argentine criminologist, developed his own system of classification. It is still widely used in Spanish-speaking countries. In 1892, Sir Francis Galton published his first book on fingerprints. He categorized the nine pattern types previously named by Purkinje into three pattern groups: arches, loops and whorls. Galton's system was officially adopted in England in February 1894.

In 1901, Sir Edward Richard Henry, Assistant Commissioner, London Metropolitan Police, basing much of his data on Galton's discoveries, published his *Classification and Use of Fingerprints*. The system was so applicable that Henry emerged as the "Father of Fingerprints," at least as the first man to apply fingerprints successfully to identification. The Henry System, with some modification, together with the Vucetich method, forms the basis for all fingerprint systems throughout the civilized world today.

In 1914, fingerprints were officially adopted in France as a means of identification, replacing Anthropometry. This was a method using eleven measurements of the human body founded by Alphonse Bertillon. In 1903, fingerprinting was officially adopted by the State of New York, Department of Prisons. In 1904, the city of St. Louis, Missouri Police Department officially adopted the Henry System of fingerprints, becoming the first police department in the United States to do so.

In 1908, the FBI's Bureau of Identification had its inception and in 1924, by an act of Congress, officially established a Bureau of Identification. Fingerprint records from Leavenworth Penitentiary and the International Association of Chiefs of Police were combined and added to the Federal Bureau which now includes the largest single collection of fingerprints in the world.

For many years fingerprints have played an invaluable role in criminal and investigative work. For centuries man has utilized various systems of identification such as branding, tattooing, distinctive clothing, photography and measurement (Bertillon System). These systems, without exception, have not produced completely desirable results. Only fingerprinting, of all methods of identification, has proved to be both infallible and feasible.

Criminal identification by means of fingerprints is one of the most powerful factors in obtaining the apprehension of fugitives who might otherwise escape arrest and continue their criminal activities. The peace officer is enabled not only to locate dangerous and badly wanted criminals, but to secure complete and accurate information about a prisoner's previous criminal history and to solve cases which previously have baffled the best investigative techniques.

The FBI's identification division, founded in 1924, possesses the largest collection of fingerprints in the world. They are divided into criminal and non-criminal files. The non-criminal files contain fingerprints of members of the armed forces, government employees, and persons who have voluntarily had their prints recorded as a permanent means of identification. The latter group includes private citizens, club members, Boy Scouts, and others interested in the science of fingerprinting.

The identification division of the FBI has steadily increased in size and effectiveness over the years. In 1924, at the time of its founding, the identification division consisted of 810,188 fingerprint cards. These cards represented a consolidation of the fingerprint collections of the National Bureau of Criminal Identification sponsored by the International Association of Chiefs of Police and Leavenworth Penitentiary Bureau. In its first year of existence, the identification division received and handled 104,660 fingerprint cards; a daily average of less than 500. By the end of the fiscal year 1942, fingerprint cards were coming in at the rate of over 114,000 a day and the total number on file rocketed to nearly 43,000,000. The peak year for the identification division was in 1943 when a total of 28,733,286 fingerprint cards were received.

The effectiveness of the identification division has increased with the volume of fingerprint cards submitted. In fiscal year 1925, when less than one million prints were on file and fewer than 500 records a day were being received, 22.4% of all arrest fingerprint cards received were identified. In 1949, with over 112,000,000 prints on file this percentage had risen to 73.68%.

Day after day, fingerprints aid police officers in performing feats of accomplishment. A set of fingerprints received by the identification division in the morning may result in the apprehension of a fugitive before nightfall. In February 1960, for example, the identification division identified 841 fugitives and maintained notices in its files on a total of 82,893 wanted persons.

The identification division serves as a national clearing house for fingerprints in the United States. In addition, through the International Exchange of Fingerprints, criminals who have fled across national boundaries can be identified and located. In fiscal year 1949, the FBI maintained an exchange with 79 foreign countries and territorial possessions. A total of 13,975 fingerprint records were exchanged. The FBI succeeded in identifying, with previous records, 23.89% of the fingerprint cards received from outside the country. Approximately 11% of those transmitted from this country were identified by the recipients with records previously on file.

In addition to their criminal functions, fingerprints serve many humanitarian purposes. For example, they aid in the location of missing persons absent from their homes for many years; the identification of amnesia victims; the identification of mutilated bodies of servicemen killed in action and unidentifiable by any other means; and the determination of the identities of victims, otherwise unidentifiable, of airplane crashes, railroad wrecks, or disasters by fire, explosion and accident.

What does a Fingerprint Prove?

First of all, we know that fingers can be long or short, fat or skinny. They are used for scratching, for holding, for caressing, and for feeling. They are also sensitive to heat and cold. They belong to the rich, the poor, the talented and the beggar. When given in a handshake, they symbolize friendship.

Fingers are also used in the commission of crimes, and now, instead of being used as listed above, they become instruments to kill, burglarize, thieve, burn and rob. Nonetheless, they all leave their own calling card in the form of a print. For years, investigators knew of the print, but never knew how to use them because they all looked the same to the unskilled observer.

The Supreme Court of California in a 1946 ruling stated, "fingerprints are the strongest evidence to prove the identity of a person." Fingerprints are considered to be *direct evidence*, and are the best evidence which can be used in those cases where a positive identification is necessary.

The fingerprint proves that the person to whom the print belongs was at the location where the print was found. A fingerprint expert will testify in court that he lifted the print from a certain location. He will also testify regarding any comparison he has made and the opinion he has reached. From this point on, it is the responsibility of the defense to explain how the print in question happened to be where it was found. That is why, in many cases, the defense will stipulate to the testimony of the fingerprint expert.

What is a Fingerprint?

The fingers, palms of the hands, toes, and the soles of the feet are covered with tiny lines known as friction ridges. These ridges create friction and make it easier for us to hold small objects. These ridges appear on the fetus between 100 and 120 days after conception. They are one of the first forms of life that the human body takes on before birth, and one of the last to disappear after death. There is no change in these ridges throughout life, except for normal growth and permanent scarring. Many attempts have been made by criminals to change their fingerprint classification. However, none have been successful.

History of Classification

A fingerprint classification is a formula given to a complete set of ten fingers as they appear on a fingerprint card generally based on pattern type, ridge count, or ridge tracing. The fingerprint classification could be referred to as the "alphabet" by which fingerprint cards are filed in a location where, at some future time, they can be located. Since fingerprints do not change throughout life, neither does the classification. Each time the fingerprint card is classified, it yields the same classification.

Many questions are asked about family trends in fingerprint patterns. As far as it is known, no information has ever appeared which would indicate that children do, or do not, have fingerprint patterns which are similar to their parents. Because of the percentage of loop patterns being greater than any other type, it is usually found that parents with all loop patterns will quite often produce children with all loop patterns.

We do have many instances where family members have the same classification. This has nothing at all to do with these families having the same fingerprints. This means that these family members have the same pattern type prints, with the same pattern type ridge count, or tracing, and that these prints will be found in the same area of the fingerprint file. The points of identification found in these fingerprints will be quite different.

As you can see, fingerprints are a valuable tool to the world and especially to police work. More is being discovered every year about the tiny lines at the end of our fingers. It is now possible to obtain the suspect's prints on homicide victims under certain conditions. Who knows what the future has in store for the science of fingerprints.

Chapter 2

Fingerprint Pattern Types and Classifications

In fingerprint work all impressions are divided into three groups: *Arches, Loops* and *Whorls*. Approximately five percent of all fingerprints are Arches, 30 percent of all fingerprints are Whorls, and 65 percent of all fingerprints are Loops.

These three main groups are further subdivided and result in a total of eight fingerprint patterns: Plain Arch, Tented Arch, Ulnar Loop, Radial Loop, Plain Whorl, Double Loop Whorl, Central Pocket Loop Whorl and Accidental Whorl. (See Figures 1 — 10).

Figure 1 Plain Arch   *Figure 2* Tented Arch

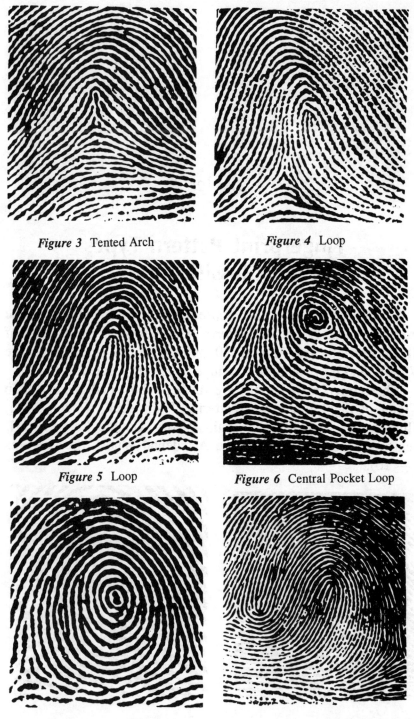

Figure 3 Tented Arch

Figure 4 Loop

Figure 5 Loop

Figure 6 Central Pocket Loop

Figure 7 Plain Whorl

Figure 8 Double Loop

Figure 9 Double Loop

Figure 10 Accidental

Before discussing the different pattern types at length, there are a number of definitions that must be covered and understood. The first of these is the *pattern area*. All patterns have an area which could be called the pattern area. Arches and some Tented Arches are said to have a lack of pattern area. The Loop and Whorl families are the patterns where we find the necessity to know and be able to distinguish the pattern area. "The *pattern area* is that portion of a fingerprint wherein we find the Cores and Deltas with which we are concerned in classifying." This means just what it says. The pattern area is where we look to find the Cores and Deltas which we need to classify a fingerprint card. Further understanding will take place as you read more about each definition. (See Illustrations 1 and 2).

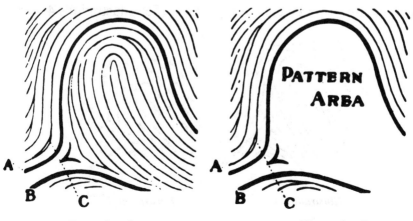

Illustration 1   *Illustration 2*

Before the next definitions we must first understand the meaning of two words— bifurcation and divergence. A *bifurcation* is the forking or splitting of one ridge into two or more branches. A *divergence* is the smooth spreading apart of two ridges which have been running parallel or nearly parallel. (See Illustration 3).

BIFURCATION   DIVERGENCE

Illustration 3

The next discussion will be about *Type Lines*. "Type lines are the two innermost ridges that run parallel, diverge, and surround or tend to surround the pattern area." Several things are to be considered in this definition. First, that the type lines are the two innermost ridges; and second, they run parallel, they diverge, and they surround the pattern area. Type lines can be several things: they can be broken, they can be short, and they can actually be continuous lines.

Type lines cannot be angular formations. Neither of the two type lines can have any degree of angle. They cannot be forks of a bifurcation. As you can see, definitions may have dual meanings. For instance, divergence, a term defined earlier, must flow apart smoothly without an angle. Also, both legs of a bifurcation can be type lines if they travel far enough to meet all the requirements of the type lines. We see that in the strict meaning of the words, type lines that began as a bifurcation cease to be a bifurcation once they have met the requirements of type lines. (See Illustrations 4 — 8).

Illustration 4   *Illustration 5*

Illustration 6

Illustration 7

Illustration 8

The pattern area is that part of a loop or whorl in which appear the core, delta and ridges with which we are concerned in classifying. The pattern area of loops and whorls are enclosed by type lines. Where there is a definite break in a type line, the ridge immediately outside of it is considered as its continuation. When the type lines are very short, considerable care must be taken in locating them. Angles are never formed by a single ridge, but by the abutting of one ridge against another. Therefore, an angular formation cannot be used as a type line. The two forks of a bifurcation may never constitute type lines. There is a single exception to this rule: When the forks of a bifurcation run parallel after bifurcation and then diverge, the bifurcation may then be considered as a type line.

The Delta

The delta is defined as the first obstruction at or in front of and nearest the center of the point of divergence of the type lines. The delta can be thought of as a location or starting place. (See Illustrations 9 and 10).

Illustration 9   *Illustration 10*

Deltas may be one of the following:

- A bifurcation.
- A short ridge.
- An ending ridge.
- A meeting of two ridges.
- A dot.
- On the first recurve in front of the divergence.
- On the end of a ridge.
- Located on certain bifurcations.

Where there is a choice between a bifurcation and some other type of delta the bifurcation is chosen. If the choice is between two bifurcations, the one nearest the core is chosen as the delta. (See Illustrations 11 — 18).

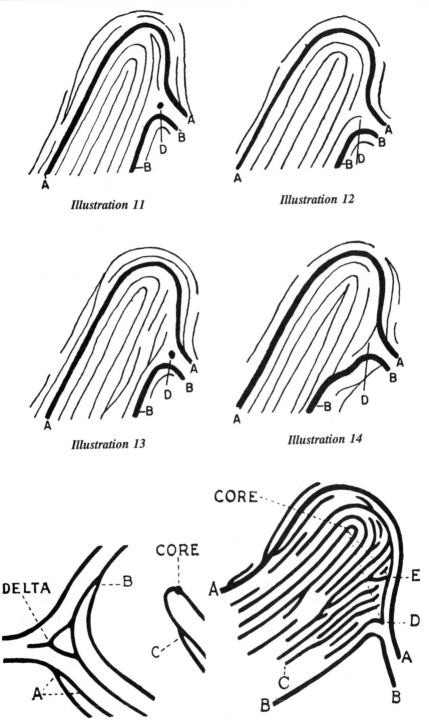

Illustration 11

Illustration 12

Illustration 13

Illustration 14

Illustration 15

Illustration 16

If all deltas were dots that were easily located and found to be in the exact center of the point of divergence, the delta location would not be so difficult to find. Since there are only a few deltas which happen to be dots, we find it necessary to learn all we can about deltas. If we know and understand the rules governing the delta selection, it is assumed that we will choose the correct delta. After you select a delta, because of knowing all the rules, change your mind only if you see you have made a mistake. Changing the delta could very easily change the ridgecount of the print enough to put it in another classification.

Although we don't all think alike, it is very possible, if we all know and understand the rules about the delta, we will make the proper selection. It is expected that a fingerprint classifier working for any identification section should know how to interpret all the rules for locating a delta.

Illustration 17

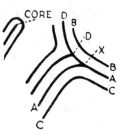

Illustration 18

General Locations of the Delta

Diverging type lines must be present in all delta formations and the delta must be located midway between two diverging type lines at, or just in front of, where they diverge, in order to satisfy the definition and qualify as a delta.

The Core

The core is the approximate center of the fingerprint impression. (See Illustrations 19 and 20).

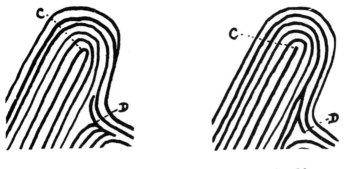

Illustration 19   *Illustration 20*

The core is placed upon or within the innermost sufficient recurve. When the innermost sufficient recurve contains no ending ridge or rod rising as high as the shoulders of the loop, the core is placed on the shoulder of the loop farther from the delta. When the innermost sufficient recurve contains an even number of rods as rising high as the shoulders, the core is placed upon the end of the farther one of the two center rods; the two center rods being treated as though they were connected by a recurving ridge.

When the innermost sufficient recurve contains an odd number of ridges as high as the shoulders, the core is placed on the end of the center rod (whether it touches the looping ridge or not). The core, like the delta, is a location and is extremely important. In the case of arches, tented arches, and the entire whorl family, the location of the core is not as critical. (See Illustrations 21 — 26).

Illustration 21   *Illustration 22*

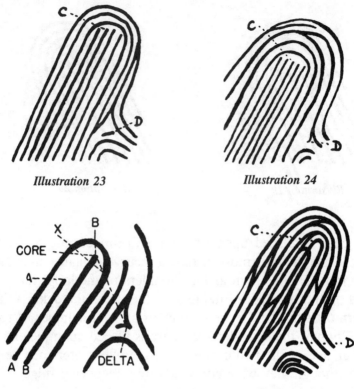

Illustration 23   Illustration 24

Illustration 25   Illustration 26

In the case of the loop family, the core location is, again, extremely important. If you know and understand the rules for locating the core you will pick the correct core. As with the location of the delta, don't let you mind be changed easily.

The core is located upon or within the innermost looping ridge. A looping ridge is a ridge that enters on one side of the finger, turns back on itself and makes its exit on the same side of the finger that it entered. (See Illustrations 27 — 31).

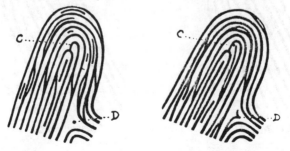

Illustration 27   Illustration 28

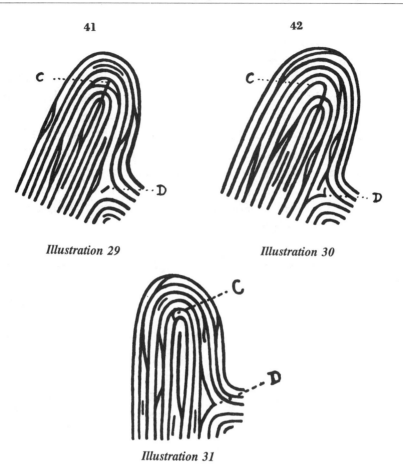

41   42

Illustration 29   *Illustration 30*

Illustration 31

The looping ridge will have two shoulders. Each loop pattern will probably have several looping ridges. However, there will be some that have only one. The core, as the definition states, is located on or within the innermost looping ridge. On or within the innermost looping ridge we may find what we call spikes or rods. To be given consideration as a core, a rod or spike must be at least as high as the shoulders. It can even touch the innermost looping ridge but must not go through. When the innermost looping ridge contains an even number of rods or spikes rising as high as the shoulders, the end of the spike farthest from the delta is chosen as the core. When the innermost looping ridge contains an odd number of rods or spikes rising as high as the shoulders, the core is placed on the end of the center rod. This covers the instances where we must select a core from rods or spokes that are within the innermost looping ridge.

The point where the looping ridges interlock can be either at, above, or below the shoulders. The following rules apply for locating the core when interlocking loops appear. When the two loops interlock at the shoulder the core will be placed at the point where they meet. In other words, the two ridges that interlock are considered to be one, with the outside legs being considered joined into a recurve. When the two loops interlock below the shoulders, the two loops are considered to be one and they are considered to have two rods inside

Locating the core when loops interlock at the center: When the two loops interlock at the shoulder or the "X" line, the two loops are considered as a single loop with one rod. The core is placed at point "C." When the point of intersection is below the "X" or the shoulder line, the two loops are considered as a single loop with two rods. Place the core at "C." When the point of intersection is above the "X" or the shoulder line, the two loops are considered as a single loop with two rods. Place the core at point "C." When two loops are at the center and not interlocking, the two loops are treated as one loop with two rods. The core is placed at "C". (See Illustrations 32 — 38).

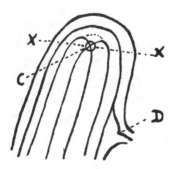

Illustration 32

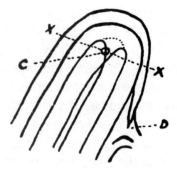

Illustration 33

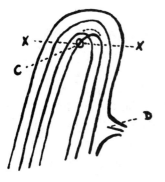

Illustration 34

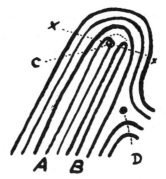

Illustration 35

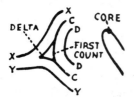

Illustration 36

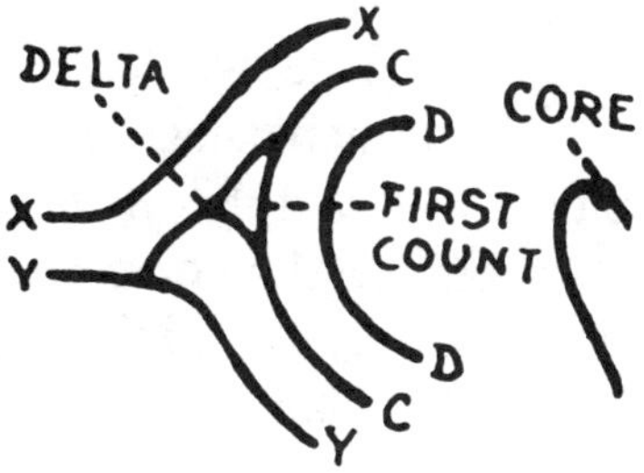

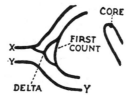

Illustration 37

Illustration 38

Sufficient Recurve

Due to the importance of the recurve, it is imperative that we know how to choose it correctly. This is particularly true in the small or minimum count loop. The choosing of a *bad or spoiled* recurve in this type of pattern will often be the difference between a loop and a tented arch (see Appendages below). When we speak of a minimum count loop we mean one that has just the bare essentials of a loop — no more and no less. In this type pattern we must recognize a smooth flow off of an appendage. We must know if the recurve has passed or touched the imaginary line.

A sufficient recurve may be defined as that part of a recurve ridge located between the shoulders of a loop. There are certain sufficient recurve requirements. It must be free of any appendages abutting upon the outside of the recurve at a right angle. It must continue on the other side or the side from which it came, until it passes or touches the imaginary line between the delta and the core.

Appendages

An appendage would be a small ridge attached to another ridge. If an appendage abuts upon the recurve between the shoulders it is said that it *spoils* the recurve. The appendage must be between the shoulders. It must be 90 degrees. More or less would be strictly an opinion on the part of the classifier. It can be placed on the shoulders. If the appendage is not 90 degrees (or flows off smoothly) it will not destroy the recurve.

Only those appendages on the outside of the recurve are of any importance. The amount of pressure used in taking the print will have much to do with how the appendage looks. Many will appear different than they actually are. We must classify them as they appear to be. The imaginary line between the delta and core is of prime importance when classifying the loop type fingerprint. The recurve must pass or touch this imaginary line before it can qualify as the innermost recurve. When the recurve does not touch or pass the imaginary line it is necessary to use the next recurve out from the core which meets all of the requirements of a sufficient recurve. (See Illustrations 39 and 40).

We have spent considerable time on these definitions and rules, but these rules are necessary to classify fingerprint cards. We must all agree, or nearly agree, that a certain situation is a fact. It is how we apply these rules to our interpretation of fingerprint patterns which will cause us to be either successful or unsuccessful as a fingerprint classifier.

| *Illustration 39* | *Illustration 40* |

The Loop Pattern

A loop is that type of a fingerprint pattern in which one or more of the ridges enters on either side of the pattern, recurves so as to touch or pass through an imaginary line drawn from the delta to the core, and tends to terminate on the same side of the pattern from which it entered.

The **essentials** of a loop are:

1. A delta
2. A sufficient recurve
3. A ridge count of at least one between the delta and the core.

The Ridge Count

The ridge count is the number of ridges intervening between the delta and the core. Any ridge formation which touches the count line is counted. If the count line crosses at a point of bifurcation, a count of two is given. Fragments and dots are counted as ridges only if they appear to be as thick and heavy as the other ridges in the immediate pattern. (See Illustration 41).

Do *not* count the *delta* and the *core*. The lighter lines caused by the splitting and fraying of the ridges or by ingrained dirt are not considered as ridges for any purpose. When the core is located on a spike which touches the inside of the innermost recurving ridge, the recurve is included in the ridge count only when the delta is located below a line drawn at a right angle to the spike.

If the delta is located in area "A," the recurving ridge is counted. If it is located in area "B", the recurve is not counted. Note that line "C" is an extension of the spike within and touching the innermost recurve. Line "D" is drawn at right angles to "C" and is accordingly at right angles to the spike. The delta is located below line "D," and therefore the innermost recurve is included in the ridge count. If the delta falls below the right angle "D" line, then the innermost recurving ridge is included in the count.

In ridge counting, before the first ridge is counted, a white space must intervene between the delta and the first ridge to be counted. If no such interval exists, the first ridge must be disregarded. [Note in Figures 42 and 43 that while the first ridge encountered by the countline is connected to the delta, there is an intervening white space and the first ridge is taken as the first count.] In Figure 44, there is no interval because of ridge "B". Therefore, the second ridge encountered must be taken as the first ridge count. (See Figures 11 — 40 for ridge count examples).

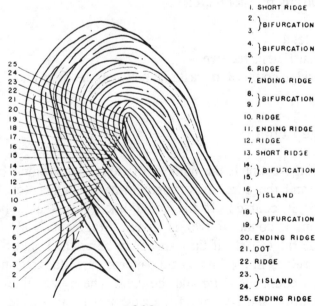

1. SHORT RIDGE
2. } BIFURCATION
3.
4. } BIFURCATION
5.
6. RIDGE
7. ENDING RIDGE
8. } BIFURCATION
9.
10. RIDGE
11. ENDING RIDGE
12. RIDGE
13. SHORT RIDGE
14. } BIFURCATION
15.
16. } ISLAND
17.
18. } BIFURCATION
19.
20. ENDING RIDGE
21. DOT
22. RIDGE
23. } ISLAND
24.
25. ENDING RIDGE

LOOP
25 RIDGE COUNTS

Illustration 41 Loop, 25 Ridge Counts

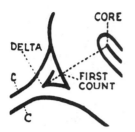

Illustration 42

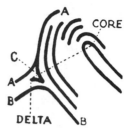

Illustration 43

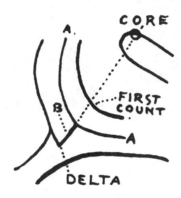

Illustration 44

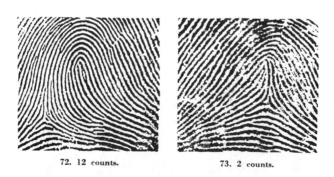

72. 12 counts.

73. 2 counts.

Figure 11 12 Counts

Figure 12 2 Counts

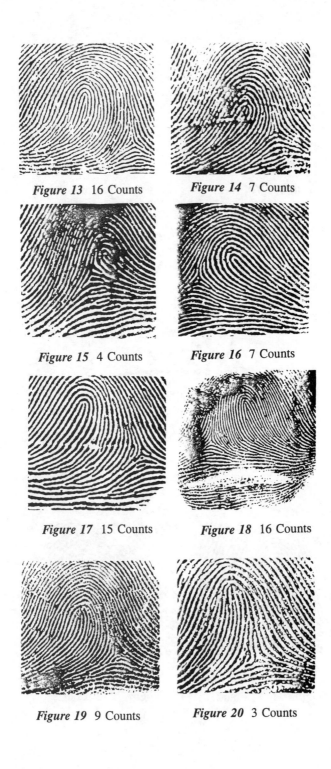

Figure 13 16 Counts

Figure 14 7 Counts

Figure 15 4 Counts

Figure 16 7 Counts

Figure 17 15 Counts

Figure 18 16 Counts

Figure 19 9 Counts

Figure 20 3 Counts

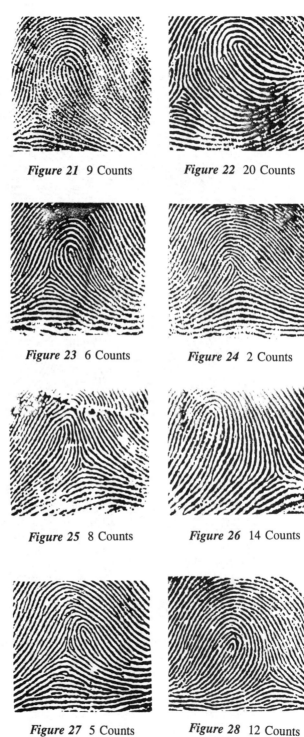

Figure 21 9 Counts   *Figure 22* 20 Counts

Figure 23 6 Counts   *Figure 24* 2 Counts

Figure 25 8 Counts   *Figure 26* 14 Counts

Figure 27 5 Counts   *Figure 28* 12 Counts

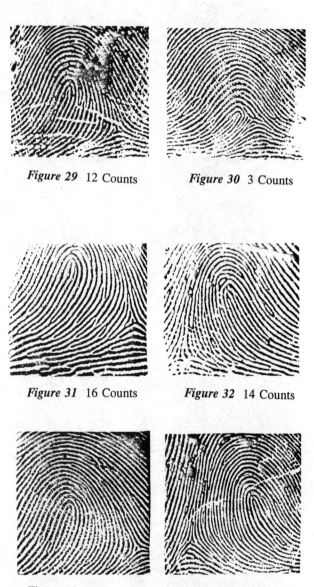

Figure 29 12 Counts

Figure 30 3 Counts

Figure 31 16 Counts

Figure 32 14 Counts

Figure 33 16 Counts

Figure 34 18 Counts

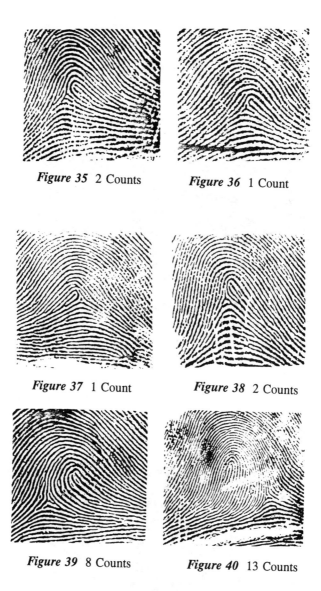

Figure 35 2 Counts   *Figure 36* 1 Count

Figure 37 1 Count   *Figure 38* 2 Counts

Figure 39 8 Counts   *Figure 40* 13 Counts

The Plain Arch Pattern

In the *plain arch pattern* the ridges enter on one side of the pattern flow, or tend to flow, out the other side with a rise or wave at the center. (See Figures 41 — 55).

Figure 41

Figure 42

Figure 43

Figure 44

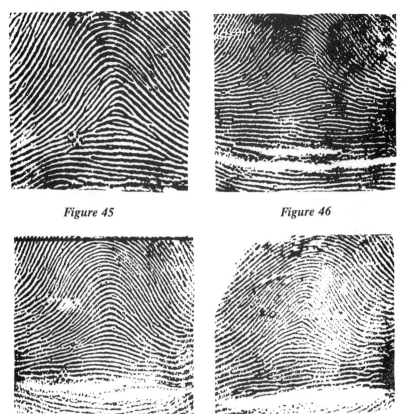

Figure 45   **Figure 46**

Figure 47   **Figure 48**

Figure 49   **Figure 50**

Figure 51

Figure 52

Figure 53

Figure 54

Figure 55

The Tented Arch Pattern

The *tented arch patterns* are the type in which one or more ridges at the center form an upthrust. An upthrust is an ending ridge of any length rising 45 degrees or more above the horizontal. The tented arch type, in which ridges at the center form a definite angle of 90 degrees or less, are shown in Figures 56 — 63. The tented arch approaches the loop type, possessing two of the basic or essential characteristics of the loop, but lacks the third.

Figure 56

Figure 58

Figure 57

Figure 59

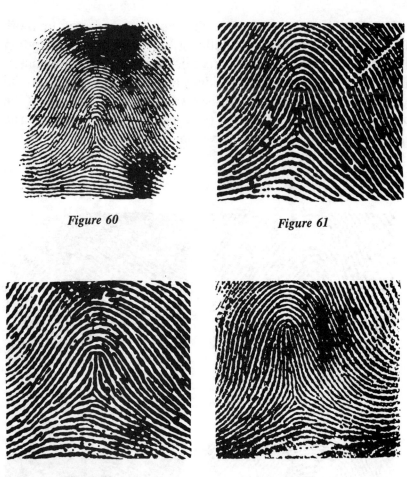

Figure 60

Figure 61

Figure 62

Figure 63

The Numerical Value Family

All of the patterns we have been studying up until now have been in the non-numerical value family: the arch, the tented arch, and the loop. Now we will begin our study of the *numerical value family*. We will discover specifically what the *numerical value* means, and its value will be covered in a later chapter.

The Whorl

We must first understand that there are *four* pattern types found in the numerical value family. Next, we need to understand that each time we find one of these pattern types we must give that pattern a *numerical value*. As we learn of these pattern types, it is very important to remember that they are in the *numerical value family*. This may sound repetitious, but it is one of the most common mistakes made in classification.

Because of the complexity and exactness of computerized searches, it is more crucial than ever before that the difference in whorl family members be recognized. In the early days of classification, before the enormous number of the fingerprint files, it was necessary only to know that a print was in the whorl family. When we consider a computerized search, the pattern type is another breakdown in the classification, just as is the remainder of the classification. With each further breakdown it is possible to makes the search that much more accurate. Remember, 35 percent of all fingerprint patterns are in the whorl family. It is important to know that a pattern is in the whorl family, but it is just as important to know just which type of whorl we have. (See Illustrations 45 — 47).

Illustration 45   *Illustration 46*   *Illustration 47*

The Plain Whorl Pattern

The *plain whorl* is that type of pattern which has two deltas and at least one ridge which makes a complete circuit, which may be spiral, oval, circular, or any variant of a circle. An appendage connected with this circuit, or recurving ridges within the line of flow, will spoil the circuit. The appendage that is referred to here is the same type that we discussed when we were learning about the loop. In other words, it must be at right angles. The location specified here is in the line of flow.

Each whorl pattern has two lines of flow. The line of flow is the area between the delta and the innermost recurving ridge. In order for a pattern to be called a plain whorl, an imaginary line from delta to delta must touch or cross at least one of the circuits. (See Figures 64 — 82).

Figure 64

Figure 65   *Figure 66*

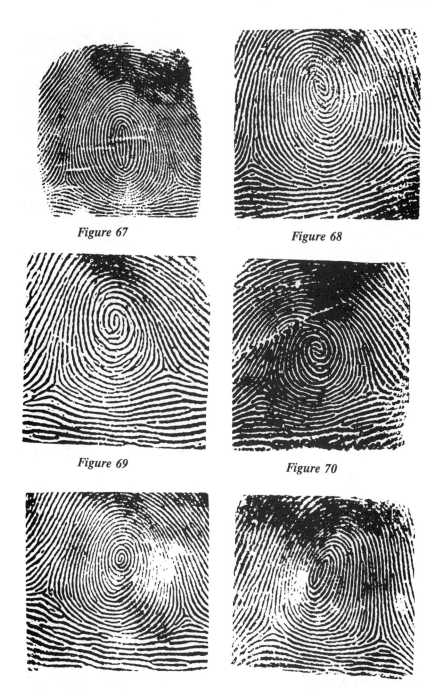

Figure 67

Figure 68

Figure 69

Figure 70

Figure 71

Figure 72

Figure 73

Figure 74

Figure 75

Figure 76

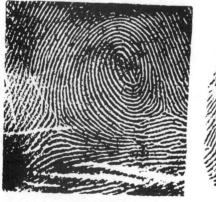

Figure 77

Figure 78

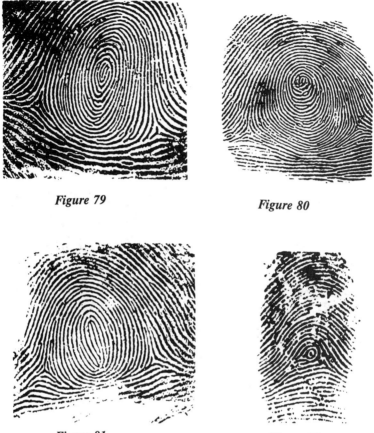

Figure 79

Figure 80

Figure 81

Figure 82

Central Pocket Loop Pattern

The definition of the *central pocket loop* is word for word the same as that of the whorl. The difference in the two prints is caused by the imaginary line from delta to delta. Remember that in the plain whorl the line must touch or cross at least one of the recurving or complete circuits. In the *central pocket loop* the line must not touch any of the complete circuits. In its simplest form this is the basic difference between the two patterns. Here you can see the importance of knowing the rules for selection of the delta, as well as picking the correct delta. Again we are reminded of the words **touch or cross**. This is another area where we need to use our straight edge on the patterns and see if you can see why the patterns are called *central pocket loops*. (See Figures 83 — 108).

Unfortunately, there is much more to the central pocket loop. The area discussed next is often very hard to understand. Usually, it needs be explained several times before it is clearly understood. I made reference a little earlier to the two lines of flow in each whorl family member.

Figure 83

Figure 84

Figure 85

Figure 86

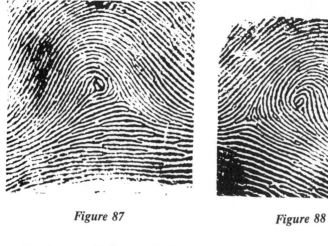

Figure 87

Figure 88

Figure 89

Figure 90

Figure 91

Figure 92

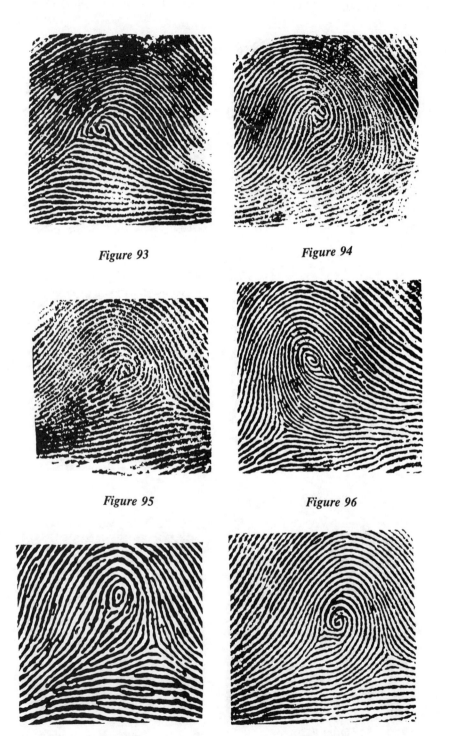

Figure 93

Figure 94

Figure 95

Figure 96

Figure 97

Figure 98

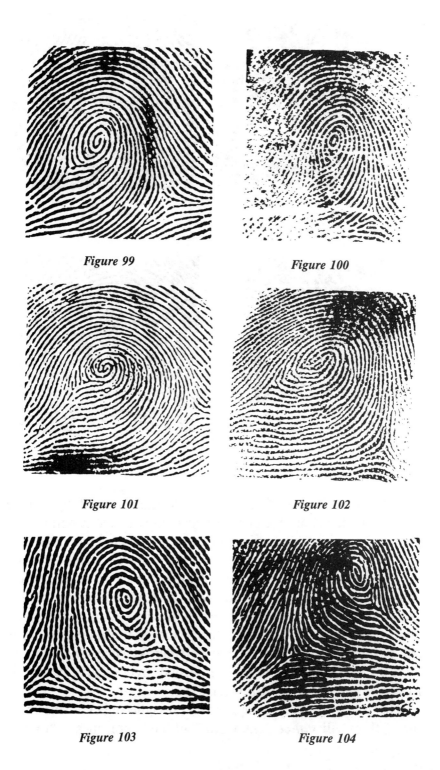

Figure 99

Figure 100

Figure 101

Figure 102

Figure 103

Figure 104

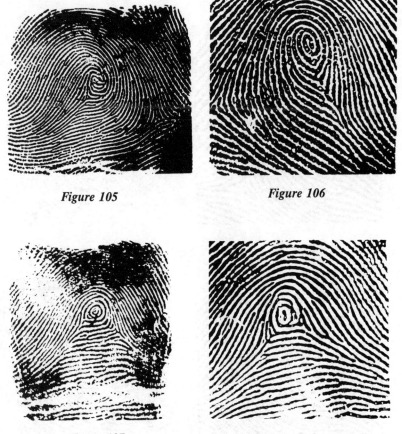

Figure 105

Figure 106

Figure 107

Figure 108

What we will talk about now is the inner line of flow. One thing we notice about the *central pocket loop* is that it will almost always have one delta that is noticeably higher than the delta. The higher delta is always referred to as the inner delta, and therefore the line of flow from the higher delta to the back of the innermost recurve is the inner line of flow. Now what we are trying to do is find something in this pattern that will cause it to qualify as a whorl type pattern. So the first thing we need to find is two deltas and two recurves. It is in those patterns where we tend to experience difficulty finding the second free recurve which is necessary to call the print a whorl type.

The rule states that an appendage at right angles to the inner line of flow will *suffice*. The word "suffice" here, means "to take the place of." There is no requirement for any specific length of the appendage. The only requirement is that the appendage be at right angles. There is a reasonable amount of information we can use to determine if the appendage is at right angles. There are many instances in fingerprint classification where we are asked to use personal opinion. This is why it is so necessary that we know and understand the rules covering these situations. Almost every problem we face will be covered by a definition. Therefore, definitions are stressed in this book.

The Double Loop Type Whorl

The book definition for the *double loop* says: "The double loop consists of two separate loop formations, with two separate and distinct sets of shoulders and two deltas." If you understood the qualifications of the loop pattern, you should have no difficulty in understanding that a *double loop* should be simply two loops, except for ridge count. What we need to understand most about this type of pattern is what will keep it from being called a Double Loop.

When we think of a double loop we think automatically of a clean sufficient recurve. The same requirements for a clean sufficient recurve are found here just as in the loop pattern. If we find an appendage that spoils the recurve on either side, we cannot have a double loop. An "S" type core cannot be considered a Double Loop because one side of one loop is one side of the other loop. There is no requirement for a ridge count in the Double Loop. This is the only area where the loop requirements are different than we have already learned. It is not necessary that both sides of a loop be of equal length. It makes no difference from which side the loops enter. In the early days of fingerprint classification there were two patterns called the *twined loop* and the *lateral pocket loop*. Since these two patterns looked so much alike, it was decided to put them both in the same category and call them *double loops*. (See Figures 109 and 120).

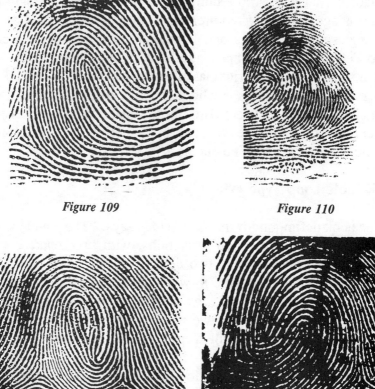

Figure 109

Figure 110

Figure 111

Figure 112

Figure 113

Figure 114

Figure 115

Figure 116

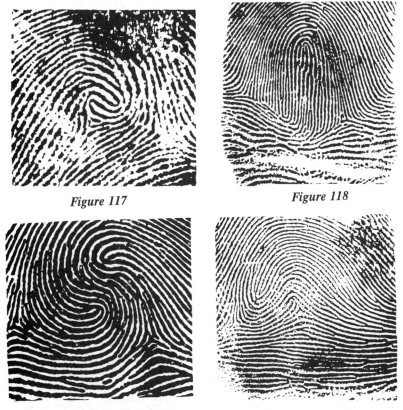

Figure 117

Figure 118

Figure 119

Figure 120

B. Secondary loop and whorl group: $\dfrac{R}{R}$ to $\dfrac{W}{W}$.

When no small letters are present, there are 9 possible combinations which can appear in the index fingers. They are as follows:

$$\frac{R}{R} \quad \frac{U}{R} \quad \frac{W}{R}$$

$$\frac{R}{U} \quad \frac{U}{U} \quad \frac{W}{U}$$

$$\frac{R}{W} \quad \frac{U}{W} \quad \frac{W}{W}$$

At this point it is well to note that it may be preferable in some instances where small files are concerned to use only a portion of the classification formula in the filing sequence. In such cases, only those parts of the filing sequence which are necessary should be used along with the final key.

III. Subsecondary: $\dfrac{III}{III}$ to $\dfrac{OOO}{OOO}$.

The sequence of the subsecondary is as follows:

$$\frac{III}{III} \quad \frac{IIM}{III} \quad \frac{IIO}{III} \quad \frac{IMI}{III} \quad \frac{IMM}{III} \quad \frac{IMO}{III} \quad \frac{IOI}{III}$$

$$\frac{IOM}{III} \quad \frac{IOO}{III} \quad \frac{MII}{III} \quad \frac{MIM}{III} \quad \frac{MIO}{III} \quad \frac{MMI}{III} \quad \frac{MMM}{III}$$

$$\frac{MMO}{III} \quad \frac{MOI}{III} \quad \frac{MOM}{III} \quad \frac{MOO}{III} \quad \frac{OII}{III} \quad \frac{OIM}{III} \quad \frac{OIO}{III}$$

$$\frac{OMI}{III} \quad \frac{OMM}{III} \quad \frac{OMO}{III} \quad \frac{OOI}{III} \quad \frac{OOM}{III} \quad \frac{OOO}{III} \quad \text{etc., to} \quad \frac{OOO}{OOO}$$

Each numerator in turn becomes the denominator for the complete sequence of numerators as listed above.

IV. Major:

The following sequence is used when loops appear in both thumbs:

$$\frac{S}{S} \quad \frac{M}{S} \quad \frac{L}{S} \quad \frac{S}{M} \quad \frac{M}{M} \quad \frac{L}{M} \quad \frac{S}{L} \quad \frac{M}{L} \quad \frac{L}{L}$$

When whorls appear in both thumbs, the sequence is:

$$\frac{I}{I} \quad \frac{M}{I} \quad \frac{O}{I} \quad \frac{I}{M} \quad \frac{M}{M} \quad \frac{O}{M} \quad \frac{I}{O} \quad \frac{M}{O} \quad \frac{O}{O}$$

When a whorl appears in the right thumb and a loop in the left, the sequence is:

$$\frac{I}{S} \quad \frac{M}{S} \quad \frac{O}{S} \quad \frac{I}{M} \quad \frac{M}{M} \quad \frac{O}{M} \quad \frac{I}{L} \quad \frac{M}{L} \quad \frac{O}{L}$$

When a loop appears in the right thumb and a whorl in the left, the sequence is:

$$\frac{S}{I} \quad \frac{M}{I} \quad \frac{L}{I} \quad \frac{S}{M} \quad \frac{M}{M} \quad \frac{L}{M} \quad \frac{S}{O} \quad \frac{M}{O} \quad \frac{L}{O}$$

V. Second Subsecondary: $\frac{SSS}{SSS}$ to $\frac{LLL}{LLL}$.

The sequence for filing the second subsecondary is as follows:

$$\frac{SSS}{SSS} \quad \frac{SSM}{SSS} \quad \frac{SSL}{SSS} \quad \frac{SMS}{SSS} \quad \frac{SMM}{SSS} \quad \frac{SML}{SSS}$$

$$\frac{SLS}{SSS} \quad \frac{SLM}{SSS} \quad \frac{SLL}{SSS} \quad \frac{MSS}{SSS} \quad \frac{MSM}{SSS} \quad \frac{MSL}{SSS}$$

$$\frac{MMS}{SSS} \quad \frac{MMM}{SSS} \quad \frac{MML}{SSS} \quad \frac{MLS}{SSS} \quad \frac{MLM}{SSS} \quad \frac{MLL}{SSS}$$

$$\frac{LSS}{SSS} \quad \frac{LSM}{SSS} \quad \frac{LSL}{SSS} \quad \frac{LMS}{SSS} \quad \frac{LMM}{SSS} \quad \frac{LML}{SSS}$$

$$\frac{LLS}{SSS} \quad \frac{LLM}{SSS} \quad \frac{LLL}{SSS} \quad \text{etc., to} \quad \frac{LLL}{LLL}$$

Each group of the numerator in turn becomes in turn the denominator for the complete sequence of numerators as listed above.

VI. W C D X Extensions: $\frac{W}{W}$ to $\frac{xX3x}{xX3x}$.

The sequence is as follows: Prints with c, d, or x in any finger other than the index fingers constitute the small-letter group. A sample of the sequence follows:

W	cWc	xWd	Wdx
cW	cWd	xWx	Wxc
dW	cWx	W2c	Wxd
xW	dWc	Wcd	W2x
Wc	dWd	Wcx	cW2c
Wd	dWx	Wdc	cWcd
Wx	xWc	W2d	cWcx

As may be readily seen, the sequence proceeds in the same fashion as the a, t, r, small-letter sequence.

VII.   Special Loop Extension used by the Federal Bureau of Investigation: $\frac{111}{111}$ to $\frac{777}{777}$.

The following is a partial sequence for filing this extension:

$$\frac{111}{111} \quad \frac{112}{111} \quad \frac{113}{111} \quad \frac{114}{111} \quad \frac{115}{111} \quad \frac{116}{111} \quad \frac{117}{111}$$

$$\frac{121}{111} \quad \frac{122}{111} \quad \frac{123}{111} \quad \frac{124}{111} \quad \frac{125}{111} \quad \frac{126}{111} \quad \frac{127}{111}$$

$$\frac{131}{111} \quad \frac{132}{111} \quad \frac{133}{111} \quad \frac{134}{111} \quad \frac{135}{111} \quad \frac{136}{111} \quad \frac{137}{111}$$

$$\frac{141}{111} \quad \frac{142}{111} \quad \frac{143}{111} \quad \frac{144}{111} \quad \frac{145}{111} \quad \frac{146}{111} \quad \frac{147}{111}$$

$$\frac{151}{111} \quad \frac{152}{111} \quad \frac{153}{111} \quad \frac{154}{111} \quad \frac{155}{111} \quad \frac{156}{111} \quad \frac{157}{111}$$

$$\frac{161}{111} \quad \frac{162}{111} \quad \frac{163}{111} \quad \frac{164}{111} \quad \frac{165}{111} \quad \frac{166}{111} \quad \frac{167}{111}$$

$$\frac{171}{111} \quad \frac{172}{111} \quad \frac{173}{111} \quad \frac{174}{111} \quad \frac{175}{111} \quad \frac{176}{111} \quad \frac{177}{111}$$

etc., to $\frac{777}{777}$.

No matter how many of these divisions may be used, the order should remain the same; and no matter how many of these divisions are used, each individual group should be sequenced by:

VIII. Final:

Filed in numerical sequence from 1 out. For example, assume that there are 15 prints in a group having a final of 14. All of these should be filed together and followed by those prints in the same group having a final of 15, etc.

IX. Key:

All prints appearing in a designated final group are arranged by key in numerical sequence from 1 out. For example, assume that there are 5 prints in a group having a key of 14. All of these should be filed together and followed by those prints in the same group having a key of 15, etc.

Chapter 6

Searching and Referencing

When searching a print through the fingerprint files in order to establish an identification, it should be remembered that the fingerprint cards are filed in such a way that all prints having the same classification are together. Thus, the print being searched is compared only with the groups having a comparable classification, rather than with the whole file.

After locating the proper group classification, the searcher should fix in his mind the one or two most outstanding characteristics of the patterns of the current print and look for them among the prints in file. If a print is found which has a characteristic resembling one upon the current print, the two prints should be examined closely to determine if they are identical.

To establish identity, it is necessary to locate several points of identity among the characteristics of the prints. The number of identical characteristics need not appear within the pattern area, since any ridge formation is acceptable. Quite often excellent ridge detail appears in the second joint of the finger. The characteristics used to establish an identification are shown in Illustration 41. (See Chapter Two).

The final and the key may be considered control figures for searching prints. They limit the number of prints needed to search a group (those prints having finals and keys closely related to the print being searched).

Due to the possibility of visual misinterpretation, distortion by pressure, or poor condition of the ridge detail of the prints in file, it is advisable to allow a margin for discrepancies. Except in cases where the ridge count of the final and/or key is questionable on the print being searched, the following procedure is used:

Of the prints within any group classification, only those prints are examined which have a final within 2 ridge counts on each side of the final of the print being searched. For example, if the print to be searched has a final of 17, all prints bearing a final of 15 through 19 will be compared with it.

Within the final of any group classification, only those prints are examined which have a key within 2 ridge counts on each side of the key of the print being searched. For example, if the print to be searched has a key of 20, all prints bearing a key of 18 through 22 will be compared with it.

Referencing

Too much stress cannot be placed upon the necessity of referencing questionable patterns, whether it may be in the interpretation of the type of pattern, the ridge count, or the tracing. The factors which make it necessary are:

1. variation in individual judgement and eyesight
2. the amount of ink used
3. the amount of pressure used in taking the prints
4. the difference in width of the rolled impressions
5. skin diseases
6. worn ridges due to age or occupations
7. temporary and permanent scars, bandaged fingers, crippled hands, and amputation.

For the highest degree of accuracy, all rolled impressions should be checked by the plain impressions, which generally are not distorted by pressure. This also helps prevent error caused by the reversal or mixing of the rolled impressions out of their proper order. For the same reason, as much of the counting and tracing should be done in the plain impressions as it is possible to do.

If there is any doubt as to which of the two or more classifications should be assigned to a given pattern, it is given the preferred classification and reference searches are conducted in all other possible classifications. For example, if on a print with the preferred classification $\frac{1\ A}{1\ Aa}$ it is questionable whether the left middle finger should be a plain arch, a tented arch, or a radial loop, the print is searched in the $\frac{1\ A}{1\ Aa}$ group, and reference searches are conducted in the $\frac{1\ A}{1\ At}$ and $\frac{1\ A}{1\ Ar}$ groups. For further illustration, a print is given a preferred primary classification of $\frac{1}{1}$, although the ridge detail on the right thumb is so formed as to resemble a whorl. The search is completed first in the preferred $\frac{1}{1}$ primary classification and a reference search is then conducted in the $\frac{1}{17}$ primary.

All ridge counts that are "line counts," i.e., when one more or one less count would change the designation of the loop from I to O or from S to M, etc., must be searched in both groups. For example, in a print classified, $\frac{16\ M\ 1\ U\ III\ 10}{M\ 1\ U\ III}$, if the ridge count of the right middle finger is 10 and the count in the right thumb is 16 (as indicated by the key), the print would be searched first as classified, then reference searches would be conducted in the following groups:

$$\frac{M\ 1\ U\ IOI}{M\ 1\ U\ III}, \quad \frac{L\ 1\ U\ III}{M\ 1\ U\ III}, \quad \text{and} \quad \frac{L\ 1\ U\ IOI}{M\ 1\ U\ III}$$

When there is doubt concerning the tracing of a whorl, it should be treated in the same fashion. For example, if in the classification $\frac{O\ 5\ U}{I\ 17\ U}$ doubt existed as to whether the tracing of the right thumb might not be a meeting tracing, the print would be searched as classified, and a reference search would be conducted in $\frac{M\ 5\ U}{I\ 17\ U}$.

If there is no doubt concerning the ridge count used for the final, it is enough to search out of the group only those prints containing a final within 2 ridge counts on each side of the final on the print being searched. When, however, there is doubt concerning the ridge count of the final, the print should be searched 2 ridge counts on each side of the two extremes of possibility. For example, if it were possible for a final to be 6, 7, 8, or 9 ridge counts, the print should be searched through that part of the group bearing finals of from 4 through 11. The before mentioned explanation pertaining to the final also applies to the key.

All prints bearing amputations should be referenced to the necessary files containing prints other than amputations for reference searches.

In instances where only one finger is amputated, reference searches are conducted in all possible classifications, including all possible ridge counts or tracings. For example, a print containing the classification:

$$\text{AMP}$$
$$\frac{4 \text{ S } 1 \text{ U III } 6}{\text{S } 1 \text{ U III}}$$

with the right index finger amputated, the left index finger being an ulnar loop, would be searched first in the amputation group for the classification, then reference searches would be conducted in the following groups in the nonamputation files:

$\dfrac{\text{S } 1 \text{ U III}}{\text{S } 1 \text{ U III}}$	$\dfrac{\text{S } 1 \text{ T } \text{II}}{\text{S } 1 \text{ U III}}$	$\dfrac{\text{S } 17 \text{ W III}}{\text{S } 1 \text{ U III}}$
$\dfrac{\text{S } 1 \text{ U OII}}{\text{S } 1 \text{ U } \text{III}}$	$\dfrac{\text{S } 1 \text{ R III}}{\text{S } 1 \text{ U III}}$	$\dfrac{\text{S } 17 \text{ W MII}}{\text{S } 1 \text{ U } \text{III}}$
$\dfrac{\text{S } 1 \text{ A } \text{II}}{\text{S } 1 \text{ U III}}$	$\dfrac{\text{S } 1 \text{ R OII}}{\text{S } 1 \text{ U III}}$	$\dfrac{\text{S } 17 \text{ W OII}}{\text{S } 1 \text{ U } \text{III}}$

All prints bearing unprinted or badly crippled fingers are filed in the nonamputation files, and reference searches are conducted in the amputation group.

For the purpose of determining if it is feasible to conduct reference searches in all possible classifications, the method of referencing amputations is applied to completely scarred patterns (Chapter 4):

$$\frac{13 \text{ O } 17 \text{ W OOO } 14}{\text{L } 17 \text{ U OOI}}$$

with the left middle finger completely scarred, the right middle finger being an ulnar loop with a ridge count of 13, would be searched first in the group for that classification, then reference searches would be conducted in the following groups:

$\dfrac{\text{O } 17 \text{ W OOO}}{\text{L } 17 \text{ U OII}}$	$\dfrac{\text{O } 17 \text{ W}}{\text{L } 17 \text{ Ur}}$	$\dfrac{\text{O } 19 \text{ W OOO}}{\text{L } 17 \text{ U OOI}}$
$\dfrac{\text{O } 17 \text{ W}}{\text{L } 17 \text{ Ua}}$	$\dfrac{\text{O } 19 \text{ W OOO}}{\text{L } 17 \text{ U OII}}$	
$\dfrac{\text{O } 17 \text{ W}}{\text{L } 17 \text{ Ut}}$	$\dfrac{\text{O } 19 \text{ W OOO}}{\text{L } 17 \text{ U OMI}}$	

The referencing of partial scars is a problem in which many factors are present. A full explanation of the scars, their preferred classifications and their references is made in Chapter 4.

When the age extension is utilized and a "Reference" group and a "Presumptive Dead" file are maintained, it is suggested that a general allowance of 5 years be considered to allow for a discrepancy on prints bearing the ages of 50 years or older.

In the files of the Federal Bureau of Investigation the various age groups are as follows:

1 — 54   "Regular" file.

55 — 74   "Reference" file.

75 — and over   "Presumptive Dead" file.

Reference searches for the preceding groups are conducted in the following manner:

50 — 54   Referenced to "Reference" file.

70 — 74   Referenced to "Presumptive Dead" and "Regular" files.

75 — 79   Referenced to "Reference" and "Regular" files.

80 and older   Referenced to "Regular" file only.

If no age is given, it should be searched first in the regular file and reference searches should be conducted in the "Reference" group and the "Presumptive Dead" file.

When separate male and female files are maintained, there may be doubt as to the sex of a subject due to a discrepancy between the sex indicated and the name and the description and picture. In such cases, try to determine the sex from the description and the size of the prints, then reference the print to the other file. A photostat copy can be made and placed in the other file until the true sex can be determined.

Chapter 7

Techniques for Taking Good Fingerprints

The FBI Identification Division has historically adhered to a policy of processing any legible set of fingerprints through its fingerprint files; however, only fingerprints taken with black printer's ink would be retained in the Identification Division files. The FBI has for many years recommended all fingerprint impressions be taken with black printer's ink to insure the fingerprints are clear, legible, and of a permanent nature. The FBI continues to recommend the use of black printer's ink; however, inkless chemical processes for obtaining fingerprints have recently been developed which produce legible black impressions on standard white fingerprint cardstock. The FBI Identification Division will now process and retain, in addition to fingerprints taken with black printer's ink, fingerprint impressions taken by inkless chemical processes provided:

1. The fingerprints are recorded with a medium which provides uniform black impressions, clear in contrast, on standard white fingerprint cardstock. If other than black printer's ink is used, the endurance of the medium must be attested to as being permanent. This certification should come from the supplier of the process.

2. The fingerprint submission emanates from an authorized fingerprint contributor and the fingerprint card reflects all necessary data.

For those agencies and departments which continue to use the tried and proven process of recording fingerprint impressions with black printer's ink, the following is offered for your assistance; however, much of the material offered is applicable to any method of recording fingerprint impressions.

How to Take Inked Fingerprints

The basic equipment for taking fingerprints consists of an inking plate, a cardholder, printer's ink (heavy black paste), and roller. This equipment is simple and inexpensive.

In order to obtain clear, distinct fingerprints, it is necessary to spread the printer's ink in a thin, even coating on a small inking plate. A roller similar to that used by printers in making gallery proofs is best adapted for use as a spreader. Its size is a matter determined by individual needs and preferences. However, a roller approximately 3 inches long and 1 inch in diameter has been found to be very satisfactory. These rollers may be obtained from a fingerprint supply company or a printing supply house.

An inking plate may be made from a hard, rigid, scratch-resistant metal plate 6 inches wide by 14 inches long or by inlaying a block of wood with a piece of glass one-forth of an inch thick, 6 inches wide, and 14 inches long. The glass plate by itself would be suitable, but it should be fixed to a base in order to prevent breaking. The inking surface should be elevated to a sufficient height to allow the subject's forearm to assume a horizontal position when the fingers are being inked. For example, the inking plate may be placed on the edge of a counter or a table of counter height. In such a position, the operator has greater assurance of avoiding accidental strain or pressure on the fingers and should be able to procure more uniform impressions. The inking plate should also be placed so that the subject's fingers which are not being printed can be made to "swing" off the table to prevent their interfering with the inking process.

A fingerprint stand may be purchased from fingerprint supply companies. The stand is made of hardwood and measures approximately 2 feet in length, 1 foot in height and width. This stand contains a cardholder and a chrome strip which is used as the inking plate. Two compartments used to store blank fingerprint cards and supplies complete the stand. This equipment should be supplemented by a cleansing fluid and necessary cloths so that the subject's fingers may be cleaned before rolling and the inking plate cleaned after using. Denatured alcohol and commercially available fluids are suitable for this purpose.

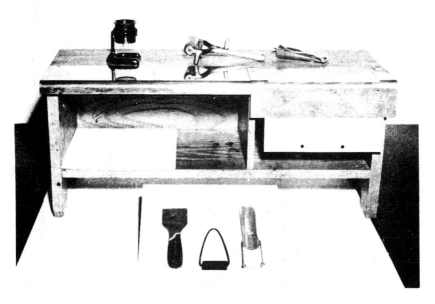

Fingerprint Stand

The fingerprints should be taken on 8 by 8 inch cardstock, as this size has generally been adopted by law enforcement agencies due to the facility in filing and desirability of uniformity. Figure 144 shows fingerprints properly taken on one of the standard personal identification cards from the Federal Bureau of Investigation. From this illustration, it is evident there are two types of impressions involved in the process of taking fingerprints.

The upper 10 prints are taken individually — thumb, index, middle, ring and little fingers of each hand in the order named. These are called "rolled" impressions. To create these, fingers are rolled from side to side to obtain all available ridge detail. The smaller impressions at the bottom of the card are taken by simultaneously printing all of the fingers of each hand and then the thumb without rolling. These are called "plain" or "simultaneous" impressions and are used as a check on the sequence and accuracy of rolled impressions. Rolled impressions must be taken carefully in order to insure that an accurate fingerprint classification can be obtained by examination or the various patterns. It is also necessary that each focal point (core and all deltas) be clearly printed in order that accurate ridge counts and tracings may be obtained.

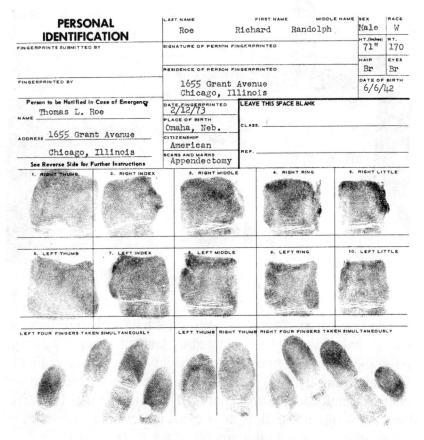

Figure 144 Fingerprints properly taken

In preparing to take a set of fingerprints, a small daub of ink should be placed on the inking glass or slab and thoroughly rolled until a very thin, even film covers the entire surface. The subject should stand in front of and at forearm's length from the inking plate. In taking the rolled impressions, the side of the bulb of the finger is placed on the inking plate and the finger is rolled to the other side until it faces the opposite direction. Care should be exercised so the bulb of each finger is inked evenly from the tip to below the first joint.

By pressing the finger lightly on the card and rolling in exactly the same manner, a clear rolled impression of the finger surface may be obtained. It is better to ink and print each finger separately beginning with the right thumb and then, in order, the index, middle, ring, and little fingers (stamp pad ink, printing ink, ordinary writing ink, or other colored inks are not suitable for use in fingerprint work as they are too light or thin and do not dry as quickly.)

Consideration must be given to the anatomical or bony structure of the forearm when taking rolled impressions in order to obtain more uniform impressions. The two principal bones of the forearm are known as the radius and the ulna, the former being on the thumb side and the latter being on the little finger side of the arm. As suggested by its name, the radius bone revolves freely about the ulna as a spoke of a wheel about the hub. In order to take advantage of the natural movement in making finger impressions, the hand should be rotated from the awkward to the easy position. This requires that the thumbs be rolled toward and the fingers away from the center of the subject's body. This process relieves strain and leaves the fingers relaxed upon completion of rolling so that they may be lifted easily from the card without danger of slipping which smudges and blurs the prints. Figures 145 and 146 show the proper method of holding a finger for inking and printing a rolled impression.

The degree of pressure to be exerted in inking and taking rolled impressions is important, and this may best be determined through experience and observation. It is quite important, however, that the subject be cautioned to relax and refrain from trying to help the operator by exerting pressure as this prevents the operator from gauging the amount of pressure needed.

A method which is helpful in effecting the relaxation of a subject's hand is that of instructing him to look at some distant object and not to look at his hands. The person taking the fingerprints should stand to the left of the subject when printing the right hand and vice versa for the left. In any case, the positions of both subject and operator should be natural and relaxed if the best fingerprints are to be obtained.

To obtain "plain" impressions, all the fingers of the right hand should be pressed lightly upon the inking plate, then pressed simultaneously upon the lower right hand corner of the card in the space provided. The left hand should be similarly printed, and the thumbs of both hands should be inked and printed, without rolling, in the space provided. Figures 147 and 148 show the correct method of taking plain impressions of the fingers and thumbs.

Figure 145 Proper method of holding finger

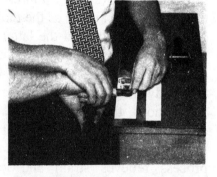

Figure 146 Proper method of printing rolled impressions

Figure 147 Proper method of taking plain impressions of fingers

Figure 148 Proper method of taking plain impressions of thumbs

Chapter 8

Problems in Taking
Inked Fingerprints

From time to time various problems arise concerning the taking of inked impressions. It is believed that these problems can be divided into four phases:

- Mechanical operation

- Temporary disabilities

- Permanent disabilities

- General

Mechanical Operation

In order to take good fingerprints, the necessary equipment should be maintained in a neat and orderly manner at all times.

Indistinct or illegible prints are usually caused by one or more of the following factors:

1. Failure to reproduce the focal points (deltas and cores) because the finger has not been fully rolled from one side to the other, and the bulb of the finger from joint to tip has not been completely inked.

2. Allowing the fingers to slip or twist will result in smears, blurs, and false-appearing patterns. The fingers should be held securely, but with the technician not applying too much pressure. The subject should be instructed not to try to help and to remain passive throughout the fingerprinting procedure.

3. The use of writing or similar ink resulting in impressions that are too light and faint or in which the ink has run, obliterating the ridge detail. The best results will be obtained by using heavy black printer's ink, which should not be thinned before using. This ink will dry quickly and will not blur or smear with handling.

4. Failure to thoroughly clean the fingers or inking apparatus of foreign substances and perspiration, causing the appearance of false markings and the disappearance of ridge characteristics. Alcohol or a nonflammable cleaning agent may be used. In warm weather, each finger should be wiped dry of perspiration before inking and printing the fingers.

5. The use of too much ink, obliterating or obscuring the ridges. If printer's ink is used, a small amount of ink applied to the inking plate will suffice for several sets of prints. It should be spread to a thin, even film by rolling the ink over the plate by means of the roller.

6. Insufficient ink will result in ridges too light and faint to be counted or traced.

Figures 149 through 160 show the results of these faults and show the same fingers taken in the proper manner.

Figure 149 Improper

Figure 150 Proper

Figure 151 Improper

Figure 152 Proper

Illegible Inked Prints

A brief review of the problems of classifying and filing a fingerprint card in the FBI will help to clarify the FBI's policy concerning the processing of improperly printed fingerprints.

Figure 153 Improper

Figure 154 Proper

Figure 155 Improper

Figure 156 Proper

The criminal fingerprint file contains the fingerprints of millions of individuals. The complete classification formula is used. To obtain it, each inked finger must show all the essential characteristics. Because of the immense volume of prints it has become necessary to extend the normal classification formula.

To illustrate this point:

dWdwc

xCdwc

O 32 W OOO 18

I 32 W III

In order to subdivide the 32 over 32 primary still further, the ridge count of the whorl of the right little finger is used to obtain a final classification. The extension above the normal classification formula indicates that each whorl is classified as to the type; namely, plain whorl (W), double loop (D), central pocket loop (C), and accidental (X). Accordingly, it is not enough for the FBI Identification Division to ascertain the general whorl pattern type, but the deltas and core must show in order to obtain the ridge tracing, the type of whorl, and also, in some instances, the ridge count. The complex WCDX extension is outlined in Chapter 6.

An examination of Figure 155 shows that it is a whorl. In order to classify the ridge tracing accurately, however, so that the fingerprint card can be placed in the correct classification, the left delta must show. The approximate ridge tracing for the whorl in Figure 155 would be **meeting**. An examination of the properly taken fingerprint in Figure 156 indicates that the correct ridge tracing is **inner**. It follows that the pattern in Figure 155 would not have been placed in the proper place in file.

The correct whorl tracing is needed to obtain the complete sub-secondary and the major classifications.

It may be noted that both deltas are present in Figure 157. This would enable the technical expert to ascertain the correct ridge tracing, **outer**. In the core of the whorl, however, there is a heavy amount of ink which makes it impossible to determine the type of whorl with any degree of accuracy. Actually, the correct type of whorl, a double loop, is clearly visible in Figure 158.

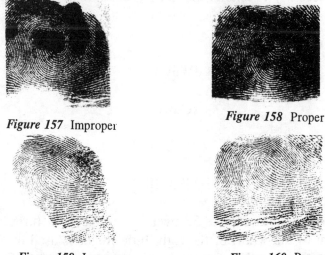

Figure 157 Improper

Figure 158 Proper

Figure 159 Improper

Figure 160 Proper

It can be ascertained that the pattern in Figure 159 is a loop, but an accurate ridge count cannot be obtained because the left delta does not appear. The approximate ridge count of this loop is 14 to 16. This approximate is sufficient for a fingerprint expert to place this loop in the "O" group of any finger of the sub-secondary. The correct ridge count of this loop is 19, and it appears in Figure 160. The approximate ridge count is not sufficient to place this print properly in the large files of the FBI because in certain general complete classification formulas the accurate ridge count is needed to obtain an extension. These extensions use a smaller grouping of ridge counts to form a valuation table, and in this way, differ from the larger grouping of ridge counts which form the basis of the sub-secondary classification. These are called the second sub-secondary and the special loop extension.

There are two additional points which illustrate the FBI's need for the delta, ridges, and core to show clearly in loops. First, the ridge count of the loop may be needed to obtain the key classification. The key classification is an actual ridge count, and no valuation table is used to obtain a subdivision. The key classification is used as an integral part of the fingerprinting filing system. Second, the ridge count may be needed to obtain the final classification. The final classification is an actual ridge count, and no valuation table is used to obtain a subdivision. The final classification is used as an integral part of the fingerprint filing system.

The following are just a few examples used to illustrate the completeness of the classification formula in the FBI fingerprint file:

12	M	9	R	OIO	11
	S	1	R	IOI	
Key	Major	Primary	Secondary	Subsecondary	Final

6		17	aW	IIO	9
		1	U	OII	
Key	Major	Primary	Small letter Secondary	Subsecondary	Final

8	S	1	Ua	II	6
	S	1	U	III	
Key	Major	Primary	Small letter Secondary	(Subsecondary Extension)	Final

				SML (Second SML Subsecondary)	
5	0	5	U	IOO	14
	I	17	U	IOO	
Key	Major	Primary	Secondary	Subsecondary	Final

				245 (Special 332 Loop Extension)	
14	M	1	U	IOO	16
	S	1	U	OII	
Key	Major	Primary	Secondary	Subsecondary	Final

15	I	29	W	IOO	19
	I	28	W	OOI	
Key	Major	Primary	Secondary	Subsecondary	Final

These examples should help to illustrate the FBI's extended classification formulas for classifying fingerprints.

The larger collection of fingerprints must, out of necessity, call for a more detailed analysis of all fingerprint characteristics. A closer examination to obtain further fingerprint subdivisions is dependent on ten legible inked impressions.

The identification officer will understand the problems of accurately classifying and filing fingerprint cards. He knows there is little value in placing a fingerprint card in the FBI's rules with only an approximate or an inaccurate classification.

Every fingerprint card filed in the FBI's file is of value to the particular law enforcement agencies which rely on its being correctly classified and filed.

Temporary Disabilities

There are temporary disabilities affecting an individual's hand which are sometimes beyond the control of the identification officer. These can be fresh cuts, or wounds, bandaged fingers or finger, occupational (carpenters, bricklayers, etc.) blisters, and excessive perspiration. Children, whose ridges are small and fine, would also come under this heading. Extreme care should be exercised in fingerprinting the aforementioned.

Temporary disabilities, such as fresh cuts, wounds, and bandaged fingers, are beyond the control of the fingerprint technical. As indicated previously, a complete classification formula is necessary in order that a fingerprint card be retained in FBI files. An indication on the fingerprint card to the effect that a finger is "freshly cut, bandaged" will cause the fingerprint card to be returned to the contributor since accurate classification is impossible. In the event of temporary injury, the fingerprints should be taken, if possible, after the injury has healed. This same situation prevails with large blisters which temporarily disfigure ridge detail.

Problems resulting from the occupation of the individual (such as carpenters, bricklayers, cement workers) are a definite challenge to the fingerprint technician. When it is obvious that the occupation of the individual being fingerprinted has affected or worn the ridges on the tips of the fingers to the point where it is difficult to obtain legible fingerprints, consideration should be given to the use of softening agents (oils or creams) or fingerprinting at a later date when the ridges have had an opportunity to re-form. It is possible, in many instances, to obtain legible fingerprints where the ridges are worn by using a very small amount of ink on the inking plate.

Excessive perspiration will result in the failure of ink to adhere properly to the tips of the fingers. When this situation is encountered, the subject's fingers should be individually wiped clean and immediately inked and printed. This process should be followed with each finger. It is also helpful to wipe the fingers with alcohol or some other drying agent which will temporarily reduce the amount of perspiration and thus permit the technician to obtain clear, legible fingerprint impressions.

In all the above situations, if it is not possible to accurately classify and file the fingerprint card, the name appearing on the card will be searched in the alphabetical files and then returned to the law enforcement agency.

Permanent Disabilities

Another phase involves permanent disabilities which can, in most cases, be controlled by the identification officer. These can be lack of fingers (born without), amputation, crippled fingers (bent, broken), deformities (webbed, extra fingers), and old age.

With respect to lack of fingers, it should be noted that some individuals are born without certain fingers. The notation "missing" is not satisfactory because it does not sufficiently explain the correct situation. It is suggested that "missing at birth" or some similar notation be made in the individual fingerprint block on the card. A proper notation concerning this situation will prevent the fingerprint card from being returned. Figures 161 and 162 illustrate temporary and permanent disabilities.

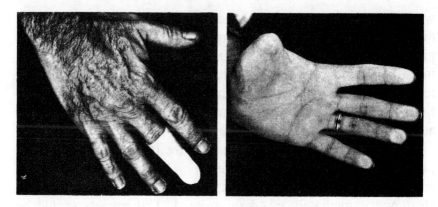

Figure 161 Temporary disability   **Figure 162** Permanent disability

Concerning amputations, it is suggested that a proper notation to this effect appear in the individual fingerprint block or blocks. It is suggested that if a portion of the first joint of a finger is amputated, the finger should be inked and printed. A notation concerning this fact should be made on the fingerprint card in the individual fingerprint block.

The handling of crippled fingers and certain deformities can be discussed in a group because they generally present the same problems. It is not sufficient in all cases to indicate "broken," "bent," or "crippled." If the fingers are bent or crippled so that they are touching the palm and cannot be moved, a notation to this effect should be in the fingerprint card in the proper individual fingerprint block. However, it is believed that these extreme cases are rare. It is suggested that the special inking devices be used for taking the prints of deceased individuals and for bent or crippled fingers (See Figure 163).

This equipment, which will be discussed more fully in the section on printing deceased persons, consists of a spatula, small roller, and a curved holder for the individual finger block. Figure 163 shows the spatula, roller, and curved holder. It should be further noted in Figure 163 that there is a strip of the entire hand of the fingerprint card and also individual finger blocks cut from the fingerprint card. Each of these types can be used in connection with the curved holder.

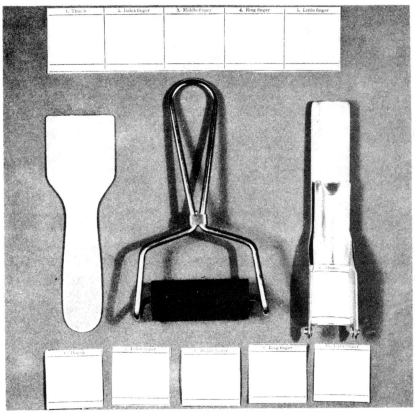

Figure 163 The spatula, roller, and curved holder used for taking the inked prints of bent or crippled fingers

Each crippled finger is taken as a separate unit and then the finger block pasted on a fingerprint card. In Figure 164, note the use of the spatula for applying the ink to a bent or crippled finger; and in Figure 165, observe the use of the curved holder for taking the "rolled" impression of a bent or crippled finger.

Old age has been placed under permanent disability only for discussion purposes. The problem is not encountered frequently in taking the fingerprints of individuals who are arrested. The situation of crippled fingers due to old age may be met, and it can be handled as previously suggested. In most cases the problems arise because of the very faint ridges of the individual. It is believed that in the majority of cases, legibly inked prints can be taken by using a very small amount of ink on the inking plate and by using little pressure in the rolling of the fingers.

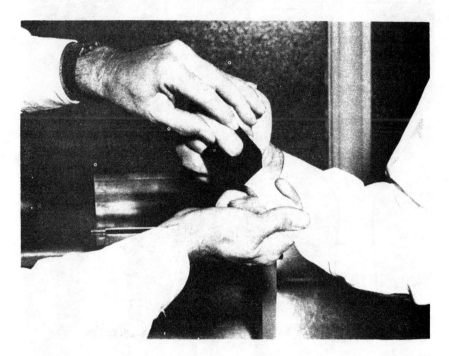

Figure 164 The use of the spatula in the application of ink to the finger

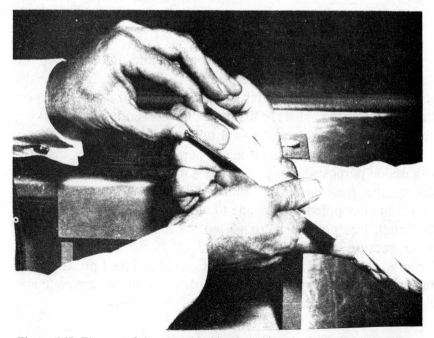

Figure 165 The use of the curved holder for taking the "rolled" impression

Deformities

If a subject has more than 10 fingers, as occasionally happens, the thumbs and the next four fingers to them should be printed, and any fingers left over should be printed on the other side of the card with a notation made to the effect that they are extra fingers. When a person with more than 10 fingers has an intentional amputation performed, it is invariably the extra finger on the little finger side which is amputated.

It also happens, not frequently, that a subject will have two or more fingers webbed or grown together, as in Figures 166 and 167, making it impossible to roll such fingers on the inside. Such fingers should be rolled, however, as completely as possible, and a notation made to the effect that they are joined.

Figure 166

Split thumbs, i.e., thumbs having two nail joints, as in Figure 168, are classified as if the joint toward the outside of the hand were not present. In other words the inner joint is used, and no consideration whatever is given to the outer joint.

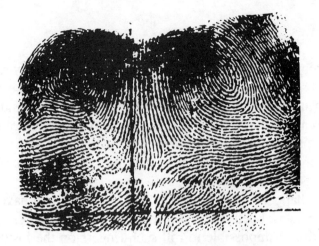

Figure 167

Figure 168

General

The preceding problems dealt with the mechanical or operational processes. However, there are other problems which may necessitate returning a fingerprint card to the submitting agency such as incomplete arrest data or descriptive information. In addition, a fingerprint card may be returned due to discrepancies in information such as name, age, sex, race, charge, date of arrest or for the lack of such data.

The success and value of the FBI's fingerprint identification services to law enforcement agencies are largely dependent on clear, legibly printed fingerprints accompanied by complete descriptive information.

Illustration 57 shows an enlarged portion of the bulb of a finger revealing the microscopic structure of the friction skin. The epidermis consists of two main layers. They are the stratum corneum, which covers the surface, and the stratum mucosum, which is just beneath the covering surface.

The stratum mucosum is folded under the surface so as to form ridges which will run lengthwise and correspond to the surface ridges. However, these are twice as numerous since the deeper ridges which correspond to the middle of the surface ridges alternate with smaller ones which correspond to the furrows. The sweat pores run in single rows along the ridges and communicate through the sweat ducts with the coil sweat glands located below the entire epidermis. The friction ridges result from the fusion in rows of separate epidermic elements, such as the dot shown on the left. Generally speaking, when an individual bruises or slightly cuts the outer layer or stratum corneum of the bulb of the finger, the ridges will not be permanently defaced.

However, if a more serious injury is inflicted on the bulb of the finger, thereby damaging the stratum mucosum, the friction skin will heal, but not in its original formation. The serious injury will result in a permanent scar appearing on the bulb of the finger.

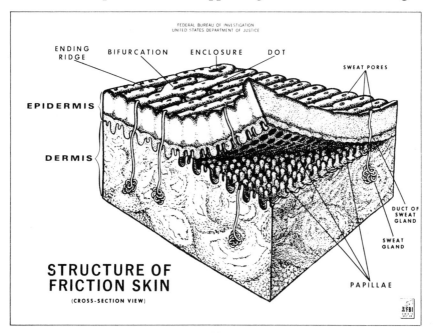

Illustration 57

Chapter 9

Proper Procedure for Taking Major Case Prints

The availability of readable major case prints of suspects and others is often critical in establishing the identity of a person leaving latent prints at the scene of a major crime or on related evidence. It is, therefore, imperative that proper procedures be followed in taking major case prints so that accurate and complete comparisons may be made in such instances.

Definition

Major case prints consist of recordings of all the friction ridge detail present on the palmar surfaces of the hands and the inner surfaces of the fingers. This includes the extreme sides of the palms and the extreme tips, sides, and lower joints of the fingers. (See Figure 169).

Purpose of Major Case Prints

Major case prints are utilized to make accurate and conclusive comparisons with all latent prints obtained during an investigation — usually a major case.

Often, numerous latent prints developed at crime scenes are of ridge areas of the palms or fingers that do not appear for comparison purposes on a routinely rolled set of inked finger-prints. Major case prints are, therefore, frequently needed to adequately compare all latent prints developed in a case.

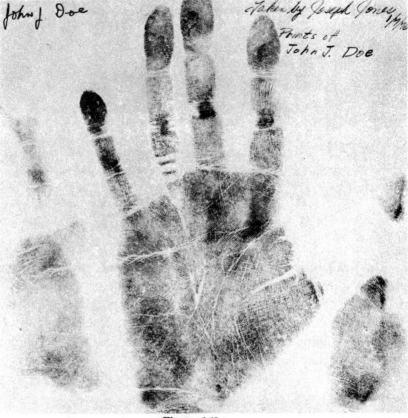

Figure 169

The taking of major case prints should not be restricted to suspects only. Major case prints for elimination purposes should be obtained from all persons who may have legitimately or inadvertently touched areas or items associated with the crime scene.

Equipment and Materials

The following items are necessary for recording major case prints:

1. An ordinary inking stand for taking regular rolled fingerprints.

2. A roller for spreading ink.

3. A tube of black printer's ink.

4. A cylindrical object 3 inches or more in diameter for rolling palm prints. (i.e., an 8 to 10 inch section of the cardboard tube from a roll of wrapping paper, a large can, or other object of this nature).

5. A Criminal Fingerprint Card (FD-249). (*Elimination* impressions should be recorded on other than the Criminal Fingerprint Card.)

6. At least four 8 by 8 inch plain white cards for recording palm prints and prints of the lower joints, tips, and sides of the fingers.

7. Denatured alcohol or cleaning fluids, along with necessary cloths for cleaning the fingers, hands, inking plate and roller.

Procedures

Caution

Before taking fingerprints or major case prints of a suspect, the officer taking the prints should give his weapon to a fellow officer to hold, or place it in a secure area completely out of reach and sight of the suspect.

The correct procedures for recording a set of major case prints are as follows:

First, record a complete set of rolled fingerprints, as shown in Figure 170.

The second step is to record the entire friction ridge area of the 10 fingers. This is accomplished by utilizing at least two 8 by 8 inch plain white cards. Prints should be recorded on one side only, and as many cards as necessary to obtain satisfactory impressions may be used.

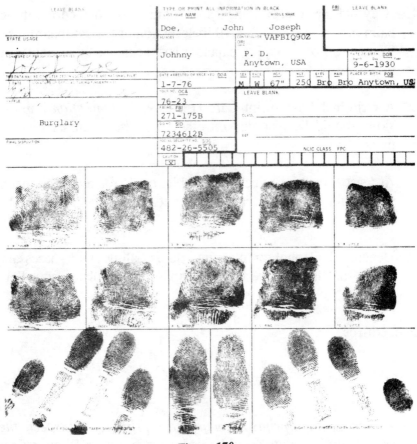

Figure 170

For best results, the fingers should be inked with the roller instead of the inking plate. The roller allows the ink to be applied to all friction ridge areas of the fingers. (See Figure 171). A plain 8 by 8 inch white card should be fastened firmly to the extreme edge of a table so as to allow no movement.

The prints should be recorded in the same sequence as the fingers appear in the fingerprint card, beginning at the lower left corner of the card of the right thumb. With a roller, apply ink to the entire friction area with the right thumb. Holding the thumb horizontally, but at a 45 degree angle, firmly press the left side of thumb onto a plain white card. Firm pressure must be applied to assure that the areas between the joints make contact with the white card. When the left portion of the thumb, at a 45 degree angle, has been firmly placed on the card, it is removed by lifting up from the palm all the way to the nail. This should assure the complete recording of the left side and tip areas of the thumb. The next step is to place the center portion of the thumb to the right of the previously recorded left side. Again press down firmly and raise from the palm to the nail. This will record the center portion of the thumb and the center portion of the extreme tip area.

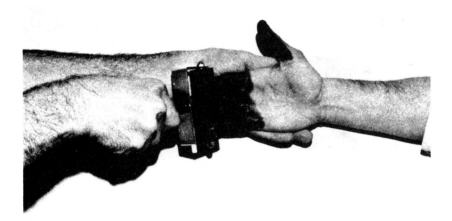

Figure 171

Next, place the right side of the thumb at a 45 degree angle on the white card to the right of the center portion. Apply firm pressure and again raise the thumb from palm to nail. This will record the right side of the thumb and the right tip area. Now, place the left tip side of the thumb at a 45 degree angle on the right side. At this time, four separate prints will be present — left side with tip area, center portion with tip area, right side with tip area, and a rolled impression of the tip of the finger.

Care must be taken to assure that the sides of the fingers are placed at approximately a 45 degree angle. Many individuals have a tendency to place fingers at a 90 degree angle for recording the sides. This will **not** result in an overlapping of the ridge detail of the other ridged sections of the finger, which is necessary.

This print should be labeled "number 1" or "right thumb." This process is now repeated with the remaining 9 fingers, in the same order as on the fingerprint card, thus completing the major case printing of the 10 fingers. (See Figures 172 and 173).

Figure 172

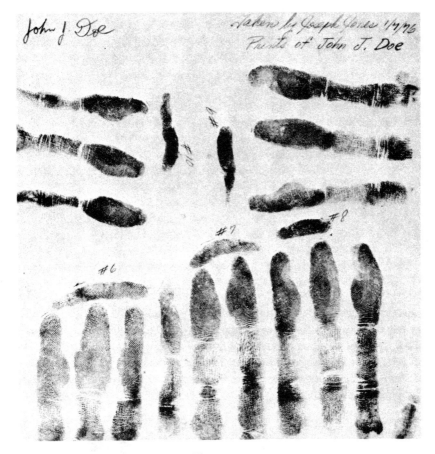

Figure 173

Recording Palm Prints

The inking of the individual's hand for recording the palm print is accomplished by firmly rolling a thin, even film of ink over the entire palmar area of the hand. (See Figure 174). This should include the extreme sides of the palm.

For recording palm prints, a white 8 by 8 inch card should be positioned around a cylindrical object and held in place with a rubber band around each end, as shown in Figure 175. This cylinder with the attached white card should be placed well away from the edge of the table. The heel (wrist end) of the right palm is now placed on the upper edge of the white card with the fingers together and pointed straight ahead. The person taking the prints

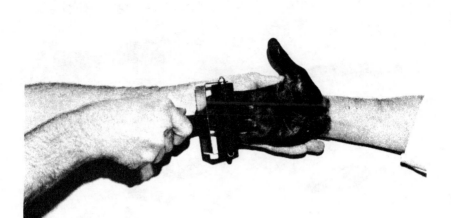

Figure 174

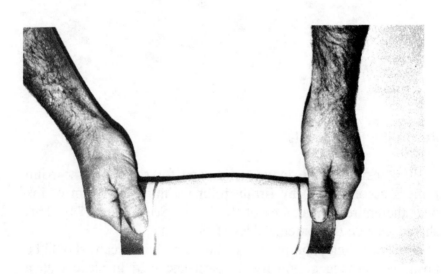

Figure 175

should merely lay his right hand over the palm of the individual being printed. utilizing sufficient pressure to insure firm contact of the palmar surface with the card. (See Figure 176).

Figure 176

The cylinder is now rolled backwards toward the person being printed until the tip area of the fingers are recorded. (See Figure 177). The hand is kept in a horizontal position so that, as the areas of the palm and fingers are recorded, it is automatically removed from the card. This is done to prevent smudging of the print. The white card is now removed from the cylindrical object and fastened to the edge of the table. At this time, the right side of the right palm is placed at a 45 degree angle to the right of the previously printed palm and pressed onto the white card. This will record the extreme right edge of the palm. Next, the left side or thumb area of the right palm is placed to the left of the main palm print and impressed there, thereby recording the entire area of the palm. This three-step process is now repeated with the entire ridged area of the left palm, thus, completing the recording of palm prints. (See Figures 178 and 179 for examples of results achieved by this process).

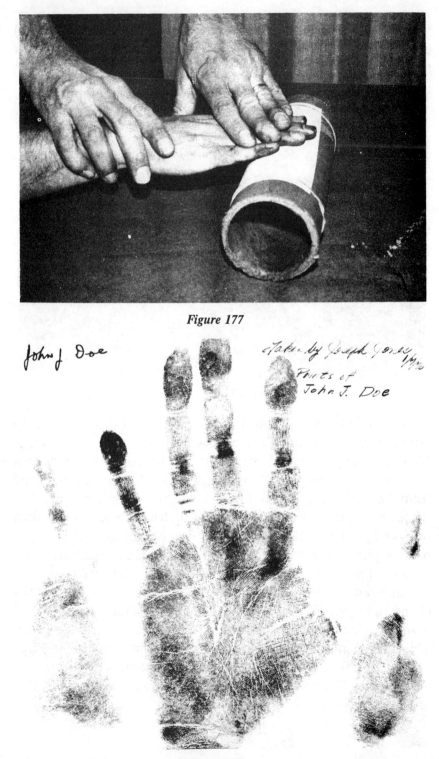

Figure 177

Figure 178

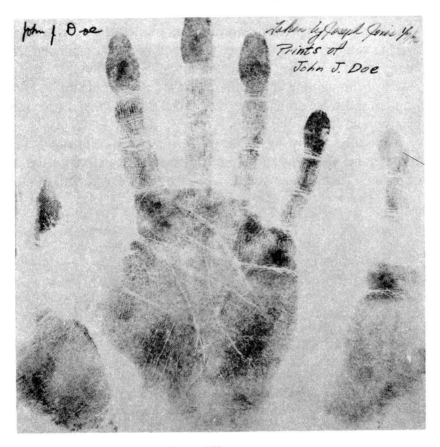

Figure 179

Signatures Necessary

All cards must be signed and dated by the officer recording the prints. The name and signature of the person who was printed must also appear on all cards.

This completes the recording of the major case prints. The individual taking the impressions will have a minimum of five cards: one fingerprint card; two cards with the lower joint areas, sides, and tips of the fingers; and two palm print cards.

A Key Asset

Clear and completely recorded major case prints can be a key asset in solving an important case. In addition to comparison with latent prints developed in a recent investigation, they can also be searched through the appropriate sections of an unidentified latent print file. By so doing, one set of clearly recorded major case prints could lead to the solution of several crimes.

Carefully following these procedures can ultimately save considerable time and effort in bringing criminals before the bar of justice. Time, thus saved, can be invested in the pursuit of other major crimes.

Chapter 10

Preparation of Fingerprint Charts
for Court Testimony

In testifying to fingerprint identification, the expert often prepares charts to visually aid the court and jury in understanding the nature of his testimony. Many times it is difficult for the layman to perceive, from a vocal explanation alone, the full importance of an expert's testimony, due to its technical nature. Consequently, some graphic representation of the facts presented is amply justified and rewarded.

The preparation of charts is ultimately the sole responsibility of the expert using them. As a matter of interest to law enforcement personnel engaged in fingerprinting work, a brief explanation of the preparation of such charts follows, along with suggestions and remarks based on extensive experience in these matters.

To prepare a chart, it is necessary to have available, in addition to the ordinary photographic developing and printing materials, a projection enlarger which will enlarge preferably to at least fifteen diameters. In the projection method of enlargement, the image is printed directly from the original negative, so the preparation of an enlarged negative is unnecessary.

In addition to photographic equipment, the needed materials are: a roll of scotch photographic tape ½ to 1 inch wide to outline the areas of the fingerprints on the negatives to be used; some stiff cardboard approximately 1/32 inch thick on which to mount the prepared charts; a tube of rubber cement; and a bottle of translucent ink, other than black or white. Press-on numbers and letters are now available at a nominal cost and are quite easy to use.

A light-box on which to view the negatives while blocking, and a lettering set to draw the lines and numbers uniformly on the charts, while not absolutely essential, are helpful conveniences. A light-box is basically a frosted pane of glass with a light beneath it to produce soft, even, non-glaring illumination. If no light-box is available, a clear window may be utilized in "blocking" the negatives.

If the expert finds it necessary to have an outside source prepare his photographs, he should retain personal custody of the evidence during the operation.

The original latent print and the identical inked print should be photographed in actual size. This procedure eliminates guesswork in enlarging both to the same degree. Whatever areas of the two prints are deemed requisite to illustrate the method of identification are then outlined (blocked) on the negatives with the masking tape, so that only those areas will show in subsequent enlargements. Generally, if the legible area of the latent print is small, it is well to show the complete print. If the area is large, however, as in a palm print, an area which will not make the chart too bulky or unwieldy may be selected.

In blocking, the negative is affixed to the window pane or light-box by means of strips of photographic tape across the corners, with the side to be blocked up. This prevents constant shifting of the negative while it is being prepared. The latent print should be blocked first. Corners of the blocked areas should be square. Care should be exercised to have as nearly as possible the same ridge formation shown and the ridge formations in the same upright or horizontal positions. This may be facilitated by fixing a negative, bearing ruled squares, between the negative being blocked and the glass to which it is attached.

If the latent print was developed or photographed as a light print on a dark background, a reverse-color negative should be prepared and blocked in order that both prints may appear as black ridges on light backgrounds. This is done by placing the original negative adjacent to a new sheet of film and exposing it. The resultant negative contains the same image as the original except that the color of the images has been reversed.

If the negative is a photograph of an opaque lift, the print appears in reverse positions; that is, (as a mirror image) and the negative will accordingly have to be blocked from the dull or emulsion side in order for it to appear in a position comparable to that of the inked print. Failure to present the prints in question in the same color and position may possibly confuse the observer and nullify the purpose for which the chart is made.

The degree of enlargement is not important in itself, so long as the ridges of the latent print are readily distinguishable by the eye. Ten diameters has been found adequate, although any enlargement from 5 to 30 will work. It should be remembered, however, that small enlargements are difficult to see a few feet away and that large ones lose some of the contrast between ridges and background. A white border of at least 1½ inches or a width equal to about one-third the enlarged area should be left for charting purposes.

Any chart prepared must be technically correct; that is, the corresponding ridge characteristics in the two prints must be similarly numbered and indicated. Several ways of pointing out the similar ridge formations have been observed, but the one which appears soundest is also simplest and consists of merely marking the characteristics with lines and numbers.

All of the ridge characteristics in the prints need not be charted. Twelve characteristics are usually adequate to illustrate an identification, but it is neither claimed nor implied that this number is required.

All fingerprint identifications are made by observing that two impressions have ridge characteristics of similar shapes which occupy the same relative positions in the pattern.

Methods involving superimposition of the prints are not recommended because such a procedure is possible only in a very few instances, due to the distortion of ridges in most prints through pressure and twisting. Such a procedure is not necessarily a test of identity.

Likewise, presenting charts with the shapes of the characteristics drawn in the margin is not recommended. Individual ridge

Appendix B

Advanced Fingerprint Technology

Because of budgetary constraints at all levels of government, law enforcement agencies have not been (and probably will never be) able to afford the high cost of the research, design, development and adaptation of improved modern technology. Thus far, with few exceptions, most of the scientific instrumentation, physical, biological, pathological, chemical and other analytical techniques utilized today in criminalistics laboratories and coroners offices were first perfected under private auspices.

Scientific research and technological development by private industry has most fortunately been adapted to law enforcement use, wherever applicable. Until recent years, only the field of medicine was commonly associated with the law enforcement and legal fields. This association was identified by the use of the word "Forensic", which Webster defines as "a science that deals with the relation and application of medical facts to legal problems." In the light of the contributions that modern technology and other sciences continue to make to the law enforcement and legal fields, it is most proper to refer to these contributions as "Forensic Technology," and "Forensic Psychology."

Automated Fingerprint Identification System (AFIS):

Automated Fingerprint Identification System (AFIS) has emerged as the latest in innovative technology to access fingerprints from a network database. Fingerprints no longer need to be manually matched to files. Time is often the critical factor in determining the success of a criminal investigation. The use of this computerized technology not only saves time but significantly increases the old accuracy match rate of 1.5 percent. Using AFIS the positive IDs compared to the number of latent prints submitted is 20-25 percent. Because of this, AFIS is rapidly being implemented throughout law enforcement agencies.

The AFIS process involves using a latent fingerprint image from a crime scene which is then enlarged and traced by hand to highlight the minutiae/relation data which serve as reference points for the system to identify when matching prints. The image is then reduced to the original size and scanned into the computer. This print is then compared to several hundred thousand prints contained in a database of fingerprints of known offenders. This process usually takes from five to ten minutes to match a print from the file. The computer assigns a percentage of probability on the matches generated. If a print registers an 85 percent probability or greater, you are almost assured this is the perpetrator. The system is also able to match imperfect latent prints found at the crime scene in a slightly longer amount of time (20 minutes). This compares to manual searches which could takes days to months. It should be noted, however, that final determination is always left up to a professional print examiner and not only the computer.

An example of how this technology was currently put to use was dramatically portrayed when California used the *NEC* ID system to match latent prints found on an automobile against a database of 380,000 known offenders. In just three minutes the system produced a list of possibles. In only two days, the primary suspect was in custody. Ultimately charged with having committed fifteen murders during a seven-month terror spree, the infamous Night Stalker was apprehended.

It is anticipated that soon this technology will be increasingly fine-tuned and networks from various agencies will be linked so that a fingerprint will be compared to one large database connected to local, state and FBI systems.